Elegant And Feminine Knitted Scarves

Gracefully Fancy Scarf Patterns for Girls

Copyright © 2023

All rights reserved.

DEDICATION

The author and publisher have provided this e-book to you for your personal use only. You may not make this e-book publicly available in any way. Copyright infringement is against the law. If you believe the copy of this e-book you are reading infringes on the author's copyright, please notify the publisher at: https://us.macmillan.com/piracy

Contents

Beginner Drop Stitch Scarf 1

Flourish Scarf 6

Destello Scarf.......................... 12

Concord Scarf.......................... 16

Jasmine Scarf.......................... 22

MissMarple Scarf.......................... 25

Berry Scarf 29

ZickZack Scarf 36

Heartwarming Scarf 39

Criss Cross Scarf.......................... 42

Cable Your Scarf.......................... 45

Elegant And Feminine Knitted Scarves

Pacific Skies Scarf 50

Fluffy Rib Stitch Scarf 53

Make It Big Super Scarf 56

Basketweave Scarf 60

Both Sides Knit Scarf 63

Hollow Miters Scarf 66

Elegant And Feminine Knitted Scarves

Beginner Drop Stitch Scarf

Skill level: Easy

Materials

Yarn needed: RED HEART® With Love® 1 skein 1252 Mango or

Elegant And Feminine Knitted Scarves

color of your choice

Tools needed:

• Susan Bates® Knitting Needles – 5.5 mm [US 9]

• Yarn needle

Gauge:

26 sts = 7" [18 cm]

24 rows = 4" [10 cm] in scarf pattern.

Project size: Scarf measures about 7" [18 cm] wide x 60" [151 cm] long.

Abbreviations

k = knit

st(s) = stitch(es)

Pattern

Pattern Notes

1. The scarf is made by repeatedly knitting 4 rows followed by a wrap row and a drop row.

2. In a wrap row, yarn is wrapped around the right needle 2 times between knit stitches.

3. In a drop row, the wraps from the previous wrapping row are dropped off the needle as you knit the knit stitches.

4. To wrap the yarn around the needle 2 times, carry the yarn from front to back over the top of the right needle then wrap it under the right needle to bring it back to the front (first wrap completed). Carry the yarn from front to back over the top of the right needle again (second wrap completed). Leave the yarn at the back of the work so that you are ready to knit the next stitch.

5. When you finish a row, lightly pull down on the scarf. This will open and straighten the wrapped loops that were dropped off the needle.

Scarf

Slip knot / Cast on

1. Make a slip knot and place it on one needle. The slip knot counts as the first stitch.

2. Cast on 25 more stitches for a total of 26 stitches on the needle.

Knit

Row 1: Knit every st all the way across.

Rows 2-4: Repeat Row 1 for 3 more times.

Wrap & Drop

Row 5 (wrap row): K1, *wrap yarn around right needle 2 times, k1; repeat from * to end of row.

Row 6 (drop row): K1, *drop the next 2 wraps off of the needle, k1; repeat from * to end of row.

Rows 7-10: Repeat Row 1 for 4 times.

Check gauge

Repeat Rows 5-10 until piece measures about 59½" [152 cm] from the needle.

Bind off

1. Knit 2 stitches loosely.

2. Lift the second stitch from the point of the right needle over the first stitch and drop it off the needle (one stitch has been bound off).

3. Knit 1 stitch.

4. Lift the second stitch from the point of the right needle over the first stitch and drop it off the needle (one more stitch has been bound off).

5. Repeat steps 3 and 4 until all stitches have been knit off the left

needle and there is only one stitch remaining on the right needle.

6. Cut the yarn, leaving a 6" [15 cm] tail. Draw the tail through the last stitch, drop the stitch from the right needle, and pull on the tail to tighten.

Finishing

Weave in ends: Using yarn needle, weave in yarn tails.

Blocking: Lightly block scarf into shape.

Elegant And Feminine Knitted Scarves

Flourish Scarf

Elegant And Feminine Knitted Scarves

Size: One Size

Measurements: Length: 94", Width: 9¼"

Materials

Universal Yarn Uptown Super Bulky (100% anti-pilling acrylic; 100g/87 yds)

• 423 Mint Green – 4 skeins

Needles: US Size 13 (9 mm) straight or your preferred needle for working flat or size needed to obtain gauge

Notions: Tapestry needle

Gauge: 9 sts x 13 rows = 4" in Lace pattern

Save time, check your gauge.

Abbreviations

dec('d): decrease(d)

inc('d): increase(d)

k: knit

k2tog: knit 2 stitches together (1 st dec'd)

k3tog: knit 3 stitches together (2 sts dec'd)

kwise: knitwise

meas: measures

p: purl

patt: pattern

rem: remain(ing)

rep: repeat

RS: right side

Ssk: slip next 2 sts individually knitwise, slip them back to left needle in this position, knit them together through the back loops (1 st dec'd)

Sssk: slip next 3 sts individually knitwise, slip them back to left needle in this position, knit them together through the back loops (2 sts dec'd)

st(s): stitch(es)

WS: wrong side

Yo: yarn over

Notes:

The long scarf will keep you cozy all winter long. Its dramatic length is great for wrapping around your neck at least one time. It features a

Elegant And Feminine Knitted Scarves

lovely, oversized lace stitch pattern. At just 21 stitches across, the Flourish Scarf works up unbelievably fast.

This scarf is knit flat from the bottom up.

Pattern

Lace

(Begins as panel of 21 sts)

Row 1 (RS): K1, [ssk, yo] 2 times, k2, k2tog, k1, p1, k1, ssk, k2, [yo, k2tog] 2 times, k1 – 2 sts dec'd, 19 sts rem.

Row 2 (WS): K2, p7, k1, p7, k2.

Row 3: K2, yo, ssk, yo, k1, yo, k2, k2tog, p1, ssk, k2, yo, k1, yo, k2tog, yo, k2 – 2 sts inc'd, 21 sts.

Row 4: K2, p8, k1, p8, k2.

Row 5: K2, yo, ssk, [yo, k3] 2 times, p1, [k3, yo] 2 times, k2tog, yo, k2 – 4 sts inc'd, 25 sts.

Row 6: K2, p10, k1, p10, k2.

Row 7: K2, yo, ssk, yo, k5, yo, k3, p1, k3, yo, k5, yo, k2tog, yo, k2 – 4 sts inc'd, 29 sts.

Row 8: K2, p12, k1, p12, k2.

Row 9: K1, [ssk, yo] 2 times, k2, k3tog, k4, p1, k4, sssk, k2, [yo, k2tog] 2 times, k1 – 4 sts dec'd, 25 sts rem.

Row 10: Rep Row 6.

Row 11: K1, [ssk, yo] 2 times, k2, k2tog, k3, p1, k3, ssk, k2, [yo, k2tog] 2 times, k1 – 2 sts dec'd, 23 sts rem.

Row 12: K2, p9, k1, p9, k2.

Row 13: K1, [ssk, yo] 2 times, k2, k2tog, k2, p1, k2, ssk, k2, [yo, k2tog] 2 times, k1 – 2 sts dec'd, 21 sts rem.

Row 14: Rep Row 4.

Rep Rows 1-14 for patt.

Scarf

Lower Edge

Cast on 21 sts.

Rows 1-4: Knit.

Lace Section

Elegant And Feminine Knitted Scarves

Row 1 (RS): Work Row 1 of Lace patt to end.

Row 2 (WS): Work Row 2 of Lace patt to end.

Cont as est'd through Row 14 of Lace patt, then rep Rows 1-14 of patt, 20 more times.

Upper Edge

Rows 1-4: Knit. Bind off all sts kwise.

Finishing

Gently wash and block to finished measurements. Weave in ends.

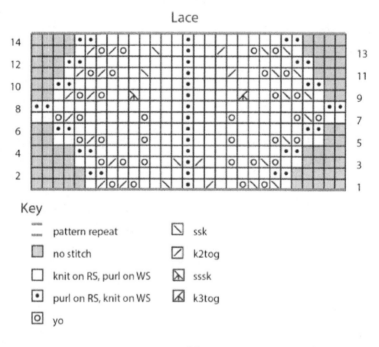

Lace

Key
- pattern repeat
- no stitch
- knit on RS, purl on WS
- purl on RS, knit on WS
- yo
- ssk
- k2tog
- sssk
- k3tog

Elegant And Feminine Knitted Scarves

Destello Scarf

Elegant And Feminine Knitted Scarves

Sizes: 5½" x 68"

Materials

Manos del Uruguay ALPACA HEATHER (70% wool, 30% alpaca; approx. 100g / 328 yds OR 50g / 164 yds): 1 sk each of MC (100g), CC1 (50g), CC2 (50g), and CC3 (50g)

Shown in H704 Beige (MC), H2150 Bing Cherry (CC1), H2121 Cinnamon (CC2), and H2110 Zinnia (CC3)

US6 / 4mm ndl, or size to obtain gauge

Tapestry needle

Gauge: 22 sts = 4" over Garter Stitch

Notes:

This scarf uses short rows worked without wraps. To close the gap between the turn and the next stitch of the row, do as follows: when you reach the gap, insert the tip of the left needle into the bump on the side of the stitch before the gap (the one on the right needle). Then knit together this pickedup strand with the next stitch on the left needle.

When working striped sections, do not cut yarn unless told to do so. Instead, carry it loosely up the side of the work until needed again.

Elegant And Feminine Knitted Scarves

Abbreviations

CC: contrast color

k: knit

MC: main color

rep: repeat

st(s): stitch(es)

Pattern

With MC, cast on 30 sts. Knit 4 rows. Now join CC1 and work in Stripe Sequence as follows:

Stripe Sequence:

*Stripe 1: With CC, k7, turn, k to end of row.

Stripe 2: With MC, knit 2 rows, closing short-row gap when you come to it (see Notes).

Stripe 3: With CC, k14, turn, k to end of row.

Stripe 4: With MC, knit 2 rows, closing short-row gap when you come to it.

Stripe 5: With CC, k21, turn, k to end of row.

Elegant And Feminine Knitted Scarves

Stripe 6: With MC, knit 2 rows, closing short-row gap when you come to it.

Stripe 7: With CC, k14, turn, k to end of row.

Stripe 8: With MC, knit 2 rows, closing short-row gap when you come to it.

Rep Stripe Sequence three more times, then rep Stripe 1 once more. Cut CC1.

Knit 1 row MC.

Join CC2 and work Stripe Sequence four times, then work Stripe 1 once more. Cut CC2.

Knit 1 row MC.

Join CC3 and work Stripe Sequence four times, then rep Stripe 1 once more. Cut CC3.

Knit 1 row MC.*

Rep from * to * until you have 12 total sections, with 4 sections of each CC.

Knit 3 rows MC. Bind off knitwise.

Weave in ends. Steam-block.

Elegant And Feminine Knitted Scarves

Concord Scarf

Elegant And Feminine Knitted Scarves

Skill level: Easy

Sizes: One Size

Measurements: Width: 20" x Length: 67½"

Materials

Universal Yarn Deluxe Worsted (100% wool, 100g/220 yds)

• 15002 Violet Rustic (MC) – 3 skeins

• 15003 Grape Rustic (CC) – 1 skein

Needle: US Size 8 (5 mm) straight or size needed to obtain gauge

Notions: Tapestry needle, stitch markers

Gauge: 16 sts x 18 rows = 4" in Fans patt

Save time, check your gauge.

Abbreviations

CC: contrast color

garter st: knit every row

k: knit

k2tog: knit 2 stitches together (1 st dec'd)

Elegant And Feminine Knitted Scarves

m: marker

MC: main color

Meas: measures

Ndl: needle

P: purl

Pm: place marker

Rep: repeat

RS: right side

Sl: slip

Ssk: slip next 2 sts individually knitwise, slip them back to left needle in this position, knit them together through the back loops (1 st dec'd)

st(s): stitch(es)

WS: wrong side

Yo: yarn over

Notes

Accessories with lots of wearing possibility are perfect for chilly months. The Concord Scarf is scrunch-able enough to be a scarf, yet

Elegant And Feminine Knitted Scarves

wide enough to be a wrap. A rhythmic lace pattern makes this a relaxing knit, perfect to work on in the evenings. Wear it however you want, and with two colors of Deluxe Worsted used in the pattern, any combination is possible.

This scarf is knit flat from the bottom up. Change colors as indicated. We recommend that you place markers in between pattern repeats to help you stay on track.

When working in the Fans pattern, do not break yarn at the end of each stripe. Instead, twist the strands of yarn around one another on every RS row.

Pattern

Fans

(multiple of 15 sts, plus 1)

Row 1 (RS): With MC, * [k1, yo] 2 times, k1, [ssk] 2 times, k2, [k2tog], 2 times, [k1, yo] 2 times; rep from * to last st, k1.

Row 2 (WS): Purl.

Rows 3-4: Rep Rows 1-2.

Rows 5-6: With CC, knit.

Elegant And Feminine Knitted Scarves

Rep Rows 1-6 for patt.

Scarf

Lower Border

With CC, cast on 78 sts.

Work in Garter St for 4 rows. Join MC, do not break CC.

Main Scarf

Note: Change colors as indicated in Fans patt.

Row 1 (RS): With MC, k1, pm, work Row 1 of Fans patt to last st, pm, k1. Fans patt will be repeated 5 times across each row.

Row 2 (WS): K1, sl m, work Row 2 of Fans patt to m, sl m, k1.

Cont as est'd through Row 6 of Fans patt, then rep Rows 1-6 of Fans patt until piece meas 67" from cast on edge. Break MC, cont with CC only.

Upper Border

Work in Garter St for 4 rows. Bind off all sts.

Finishing

Gently wash and block to finished measurements. Weave in ends.

Elegant And Feminine Knitted Scarves

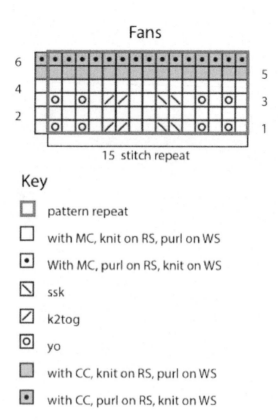

Fans

15 stitch repeat

Key

☐ pattern repeat

☐ with MC, knit on RS, purl on WS

⊡ With MC, purl on RS, knit on WS

◨ ssk

◩ k2tog

⊙ yo

▨ with CC, knit on RS, purl on WS

▨ with CC, purl on RS, knit on WS

Elegant And Feminine Knitted Scarves

Jasmine Scarf

Materials

3 (4) skeins of Purl Soho's Flax Down, 43% baby alpaca, 42% extra fine merino, 15% linen. Each skein is 219 yards/ 100 grams;

Elegant And Feminine Knitted Scarves

approximately 657 (876) yards required. We used the color Heirloom White. (NOTE: We no longer offer Flax Down, but choose from one of our other light worsted/dk weight yarns.)

US 6 (4 mm) straight or circular needles

Gauge: 24 stitches = 4 inches in stockinette stitch

Sizes: Finished Dimensions: 9 ½ inches wide x 60 (80) inches long

Notes: This pattern is worked over a multiple of 13 + 9 stitches, for example 13 x 5 = 65. 65 + 9 = 74.

Pattern

Begin in stockinette Stitch

Cast on 74 stitches. We used a basic Long Tail Cast On.

Row 1 (wrong side): Purl.

Row 2: Knit.

Repeat Rows 1 and 2 two more times.

Continue in stitch pattern

Row 1 (wrong side): P6, [p1 wrapping yarn twice, p8, p1 wrapping yarn twice, P3] 5 times, purl to end. [10 stitches increased]

Elegant And Feminine Knitted Scarves

Row 2: K6, [drop twice-wrapped stitch off needle to front of work, k4, pick up dropped stitch and knit it, slip 4 stitches purlwise with yarn in back (wyib), drop twice-wrapped stitch off needle to front of work, slip the same 4 stitches back to left-hand needle, pick up dropped stitch and knit it, k7] 5 times, knit to end. [10 stitches decreased]

Repeat Rows 1 and 2 until scarf measures 59 (79) inches from cast on edge, or until approximately 3/4 inches shy of desired finished length.

Continue in stockinette stitch

Row 1 (wrong side): Purl.

Row 2: Knit.

Repeat Row 1 and 2 one more time.

Repeat Row 1.

Bind off knitwise.

Finish

Weave in ends and block as desired.

Elegant And Feminine Knitted Scarves

MissMarple Scarf

Elegant And Feminine Knitted Scarves

Skill level: Easy

Materials:

Needle: 4.5 mm (dpn), 5.5 mm

Yarn: Rowan Lima: 2 skeins (218 yard / 200m)

Color used on pictures: Argentina, 893

Gauge: 20st, 26 rows

Size scarf: H 20 cm, L 80 cm

Pattern

Cast on 3 stitches (needle size 5.5 mm).

Row 1: Knit in front and back, K1, Knit in front and back (5 st)

Row 2: Knit

Row 3: K1, Knit in front and back, K till last 2 stitches, Knit in front and back, K1

Row 4: Knit

Repeat row 3 and 4 till you have 31 stitches.

Knit in garter stitch till 13.5 cm then change to smaller needle (dpn 4.5 mm).

Elegant And Feminine Knitted Scarves

Divide stitches: * K1, put 1 st on safety pin behind the piece * , repeat from * till * until end of row. Half of the stitches are now on the dpn and half of the stitches on the safety pin.

Rib across the stitches on the working needle by * K1, P1 * repeat this till end of row for 14 rows.

Break yarn, rejoin yarn and rib across the stitches on the safety pin (put the stitches first on the dpn). For 14 rows.

Put the 2 pieces together again by knitting 1 st from safetypin and 1 stitch from the working needle until all stitches are back on the needle (31 stitches).

Change needles to 5.5 mm.

Knit 4 rows.

Then increase every 6th row 1 stitch in the begin and 1 stitch at the end of the row (K1, M1, K till last stitch, M1, K1).

Till you have 43 stitches.

Knit 20 cm (counted after last increasing).

Decrease every 6th row by K2tog in the begin and end of row (K1, K2tog, knit till last 3 stitches, K2tog, K1).

Elegant And Feminine Knitted Scarves

Till you have 31 stitches left on your needle.

Divide stitches, change needles to 4.5 mm dpn, rib both pieces for 14 rows and rejoin (all as written above).

Change needles to 5.5 mm and knit for 7 cm (22 rows).

Then decrease by:

Row 1: K1, K2tog, K till last 3 stitches, K2tog, K1

Row 2: Knit

Repeat these 2 rows till last 3 stitches.

Cast off.

Finishing: weave in ends

Elegant And Feminine Knitted Scarves

Berry Scarf

Skill level: Easy

Sizes: Kids / Adults

Measurements Width: 10cm, Length : 60cm / 71cm

Needles: 2 4mm [US 6] circular needles

Material Madelinetosh Tosh Vintage 100g (200 yds =182m)

Gauge 21 sts x 38 rows = 10 x 10 cm in garter stitch using 4mm needls

Elegant And Feminine Knitted Scarves

Abbreviations

K: knit

P: purl

Kfb: knit into front and back of stitch

M1R: make 1 right leaning stitch

M1L: make 1 left leaning stitch slip slip stitch

MB: make a bobble

k2tog: knit 2 stitches together

skp: slip 1, knit 1, pass slipped stitch over the knit stitch

Special Stitches

MB(make a bobble) 5 st 5 row bobble

1. Knit 1, yarn over, knit 1, yarn over, knit 1 in the same stitch.

2. Turn your work and purl the group of five stitches.

3. Turn and knit the group of five stitches.

4. Turn and purl the group of five stitches.

5. Turn your work one last time and knit the five stitches together.

KNOT STITCH RIGHT

1. With the working yarn at the back of the work, insert the tip of the right needle from right to left into the third stitch on the left needle, and pass that stitch over the first two stitches and off the left needle.

2. Knit the first "knotted" stitch, make a yarn over, and knit the next stitch.

Pattern

LEAF A

Cast on 3 stitches with 4mm circular needle

Row 1 (RS): knit

Row 2 (WS): k1, kfb, k1

Row 3: knit

Row 4: k1, M1R, k2 ,M1L, k1

Row 5: knit

Row 6: k2, M1R, knit until 2 sts remain, M1L, k2

Repeat Row 5~6 until there are 26 stitches.

Knit 20 rows in garter stitch.

Elegant And Feminine Knitted Scarves

LOOF OPENING

Divide stitches: * slip 1, slip next st onto another circular needle, keeping this stitch at the back of the work. Repeat from * to end of row. Half of the stitches are now on the 1st needle and half of the stitches are on the 2nd needle. Rib across the stitches on the working needle(1st needle) by * K1, P1 * repeat this till end of row for 14 rows. Break yarn. Rejoin yarn and rib across the stitches on the 2nd needle by * P1, K1 * repeat this till end of row for 14 rows.

Put the 2 pieces together again by sliping 1 stitch from the working needle(2nd needle) and 1 stitch from the 1st needle until all stitches are back on the one needle (26 stitches).

BODY

INCREASE 3 STS

Row 1 (RS): k6, kfb, k6, kfb, k6, kfb, k5 (now there are 29 stitches.)

Row 2 (WS): k5, p3, k2, p9, k2, p3, k5

STITCH PATTERN

Row 1 (RS): k3, p2, KNOT STITCH, p2, k4, MB, k4, p2, KNOT STITCH, p2, k3

Row 2 (WS): k5, p3, k2, p9, k2, p3, k5

Elegant And Feminine Knitted Scarves

Row 3: k3, p2, k3, p2, k2, MB, k3, MB, k2, p2, k3, p2, k3

Row 4: k5, p3, k2, p9, k2, p3, k5

Row 5: k3, p2, KNOT STITCH, p2, k4, MB, k4, p2, KNOT STITCH, p2, k3

Row 6: k5, p3, k2, p9, k2, p3, k5

Row 7: k3, p2, k3, p2, k9, p2, k3, p2, k3

Row 8: k5, p3, k2, p9, k2, p3, k5

Row 9: k3, p2, KNOT STITCH, p2, k9, p2, KNOT STITCH, p2, k3

Row 10: k5, p3, k2, p9, k2, p3, k5

Row 11: k3, p2, k3, p2, k9, p2, k3, p2, k3

Row 12: k5, p3, k2, p9, k2, p3, k5

Row 13: k3, p2, KNOT STITCH, p2, k9, p2, KNOT STITCH, p2, k3

Row 14: k5, p3, k2, p9, k2, p3, k5

Row 15: k3, p2, k3, p2, k9, p2, k3, p2, k3

Row 16: k5, p3, k2, p9, k2, p3, k5

Row 17: k3, p2, KNOT STITCH, p2, k4, MB, k4, p2, KNOT STITCH, p2, k3

Row 18: k5, p3, k2, p9, k2, p3, k5

Row 19: k3, p2, k3, p2, k2, MB, k3, MB, k2, p2, k3, p2, k3

Row 20: k5, p3, k2, p9, k2, p3, k5

Row 21: k3, p2, KNOT STITCH, p2, k4, MB, k4, p2, KNOT STITCH, p2, k3

Row 22: k5, p3, k2, p9, k2, p3, k5

Repeat Row 7~22 5 times more (Kids) / 7 times more (Adults)

There are 7 (Kids) / 9 (Adults) cross line bobbles.

DECREASE 3 STS

Row 1 (RS): k6, k2tog, k6, k2tog, k6, k2tog, k5 (now there are 26 stitches.)

Row 2 (WS): purl

LOOF OPENING

Same as the first loof opening.

LEAF B

Knit 18 rows in garter stitch.

Elegant And Feminine Knitted Scarves

Row 1 (RS): knit

Row 2 (WS): k2, skp, knit until 4 sts remain, k2tog, k2

Repeat Row 1~2 until there are 12 stitches.

Row 15 (RS): k2, skp, k4, k2tog, k2

Row 16 (WS): k2, skp, k2, k2tog, k2

Row 17: k1, skp, k2, k2tog, k1

Row 18: k1, skp, k2tog, k1

Row 19: k1, k2tog, k1

Row 20: bind off

STEAM BLOCKING

Hide yarn ends. Gently lay your piece face down on the blocking board. Pin and smooth the piece. You need to pin in only a few places to keep the piece flat. Run your palms lightly over the piece to help keep everything smooth and even. Hold a steam iron over the piece about 1/2 inch away from the surface. You want the steam to penetrate the piece without the weight of the iron pressing down on it. After steaming, let your piece rest and dry for at least 30 minutes.

Elegant And Feminine Knitted Scarves

ZickZack Scarf

Material:

C1 - Lang Yarns Mille Colori Baby, Colour 51 (2 balls)

C2 - Lang Yarns Mille Colori Baby, Colour 52 (2 balls)

Elegant And Feminine Knitted Scarves

(Or any selfstriping fingering weight / sock yarn where the colour changes are not too slow.)

Knitting needle US 2½ - 3.0 mm

Size of finished scarf: ca. 0.23 x 1.60 m (9 x 63 inches)

Pattern

I have written out the instructions for clarity but in truth it really is just one pattern repeat that is knit over and over and over – eight times per row and then row by row...

With C1 cast on 96 st.

Row 1 with C1: [k5 k2tog k4 kfb] repeat 7 more times (8 repeats in total)

Row 2 [k5 k2tog k4 kfb] repeat 7 more times (8 repeats in total)

Row 3 with C2: [k5 k2tog k4 kfb] repeat 7 more times (8 repeats in total)

Row 4 [k5 k2tog k4 kfb] repeat 7 more times (8 repeats in total)

Repeat rows 1-4.

When changing yarn colour just leave the "old" yarn hanging to the back and take up the new thread. This way the edge with the colour

Elegant And Feminine Knitted Scarves

changes will look just as neat as the other edge.

Knit the scarf as long as the yarn suffices and bind off not too tightly.

Here is the chart for the pattern repeat for the friends of charted patterns

2	—	—	—	—	—	\	—	—	—	—	V	(WS)
√							/						1 (RS)

			Knit (on right side)
—	Knit (on wrong side)
/	Knit 2 together (on right side)
\	Knit 2 together (on wrong side)
√	Make 1: knit in front and back loop (on right side)
V	Make 1: knit in front and back loop (on wrong side)

Elegant And Feminine Knitted Scarves

Heartwarming Scarf

Materials

Red Heart® Super Saver® O'Go™ (Prints: 5 oz/141 g; 236 yds/ 215 m)

Elegant And Feminine Knitted Scarves

Sizes	Narrow	Wide	
Jeweltone (7195)	1	2	O'Go(s)

Size U.S. 9 (5.5 mm) knitting needles or size needed to obtain gauge.
Yarn needle.

Sizes:

Narrow 4" x 55" [10 x 140 cm].

Wide 8" x 80" [20.5 x 203 cm].

Gauge: 16 sts and 22 rows = 4" [10 cm] in stocking stitch (st).

Abbreviations

Beg = Beginning

K = Knit

P = Purl

Rep = Repeat

St(s) = Stitch(es)

Instructions

The instructions are written for smaller size. If changes are necessary
for larger size the instructions will be written thus ( ). When only one

Elegant And Feminine Knitted Scarves

number is given, it applies to both sizes.

Notes:

- To begin working with the O'Go format, carefully cut plastic tie where the ends of the O'Go meet.

- Pull tie to remove.

Pattern

Cast on 16 (32) stitches (sts) (multiple of 4 sts).

1st and 2nd rows: *Knit 2 (K2).

Purl 2 (P2). Repeat (rep) from * to end of row.

3rd and 4th rows: Knit.

Rep last 4 rows until Scarf measures 55 (80)" [140 (203) cm] from beginning (beg), ending on a 1st row. Cast off.

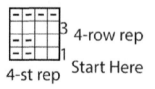

4-st rep   Start Here

Stitch Key
☐ = Knit on RS rows. Purl on WS rows.
⊟ = Purl on RS rows. Knit on WS rows.

Elegant And Feminine Knitted Scarves

Criss Cross Scarf

Materials

Caron® Latte Cakes™ (8.8 oz/250 g; 530 yds/485 m) Rose-Scented (22038) 3 balls

Elegant And Feminine Knitted Scarves

Size U.S. 11 (8 mm) knitting needles or size needed to obtain gauge.

Cable needle.

Measurements: Approx 16" x 90" [40.5 x 228.5 cm], excluding fringe.

Gauge: 22 sts and 18 rows = 4" [10 cm] in pat.

Abbreviations

Approx = Approximately

Beg = Beginning

C4B = Slip next 2 stitches onto cable needle and leave at back of work. K2, then K2 from cable needle.

C4F = Slip next 2 stitches onto cable needle and leave at front of work. K2, then K2 from cable needle.

K = Knit

K2tog = Knit next 2 stitches together

Pat = Pattern

RS = Right side

Rep = Repeat

St(s) = Stitch(es)

Tog = Together

Pattern

Cast on 86 sts (multiple of 4 sts + 2).

1st row: (RS). K2. *C4F. Rep from * to end of row.

2nd row: Purl.

3rd row: *C4B. Rep from * to last 2 sts. K2.

4th row: Purl.

Rep last 4 rows for pat until work from beg measures 90" [228.5 cm], ending on a RS row.

Cast off purlwise.

Fringe: Cut strands of yarn 20" [51 cm] long. Taking 4 strands tog, fold in half and knot into fringe across ends of Scarf. Trim fringe evenly

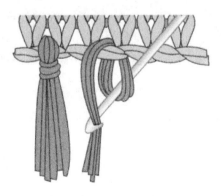

Elegant And Feminine Knitted Scarves

Cable Your Scarf

Skill level: Intermediate

Materials

RED HEART® With Love®: 1 skein 1502 Iced Aqua Susan Bates®

Elegant And Feminine Knitted Scarves

Knitting Needles: 5mm [US 8]

Stitch marker, cable needle, yarn needle

GAUGE: 20 sts = 4" [10 cm]; 22 rows = 4" [10 cm] in Cable pattern.
CHECK YOUR GAUGE. Use any size needles to obtain the gauge

Scarf measures 7" [18 cm] wide and 60" [152.5 cm] long.

Abbreviations

k = knit;

k2tog = knit next 2 sts together;

p = purl;

st(s) = sttich(es);

[] = work directions in brackets the number of times specified;

* = repeat whatever follows the * as indicated.

Special Stitches

LT (left twist): Slip next st onto cable needle and hold in front, knit next st, knit st from cable needle.

2/1 LPC (2 over 1 left purl cross): Slip next 2 sts to cable needle and hold in front, purl next st, knit 2 sts from cable needle.

Elegant And Feminine Knitted Scarves

2/1 RPC (2 over 1 right purl cross): Slip next st to cable needle and hold in back, knit next 2 sts, purl st from cable needle.

2/2 LC (2 over 2 left cross): Slip next 2 sts to cable needle and hold in front, knit next 2 sts, knit 2 sts from cable needle.

M1 (make 1): Lift strand between needles to left-hand needle and knit strand through the back loop, twisting it to prevent a hole.

Pattern

Cast on 30 sts.

Work in Garter St. (knit every row) for 4 rows.

Begin Cable Pattern

Row 1 (Right Side): K3, place marker, p1, k2, p4, (k1, m1) twice, p6, (k1, m1) twice, p4, k2, p1, place marker, k3——34 sts.

Row 2 (and all even Wrong Side rows): K3, knit the knit sts and purl the purl sts inside the 2 markers, k3.

Row 3: K3, p1, LT, p4, 2/2 LC, p6, 2/2 LC, p4, LT, p1, k3.

Row 5: K3, p1, k2, p3, 2/1 RPC, 2/1 LPC, p4, 2/1 RPC, 2/1 LPC, p3, k2, p1, k3.

Row 7: K3, p1, LT, [p2, 2/1 RPC, p2, 2/1 LPC] twice, p2, LT, p1, k3.

Row 9: K3, p1, k2, p1, [2/1 RPC, p4, 2/1 LPC] twice, p1, k2, p1, k3.

Row 11: K3, p1, LT, p1, k2, p6, 2/2 LC, p6, k2, p1, LT, p1, k3.

Row 13: K3, p1, k2, p1, [2/1 LPC, p4, 2/1 RPC] twice, p1, k2, p1, k3.

Row 15: K3, p1, LT, [p2, 2/1 LPC, p2, 2/1 RPC] twice, p2, LT, p1, k3.

Row 17: K3, p1, k2, p3, 2/1 LPC, 2/1 RPC, p4, 2/1 LPC, 2/1 RPC, p3, k2, p1, k3.

Repeat Rows 2–17 until piece measures 59" [149 cm] ending with a wrong side row.

Next Row: K10, [k2tog] twice, k6, [k2tog] twice, k10 – 30 sts.

Work 3 more rows in Garter St. (knit every row). Bind off.

FINISHING

Weave in all ends.

See schematic on next page

Elegant And Feminine Knitted Scarves

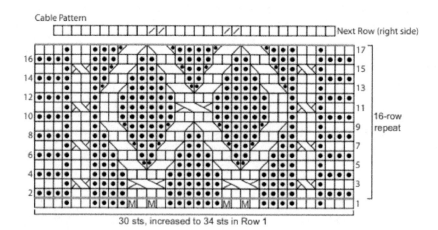

30 sts, increased to 34 sts in Row 1

Key
- ☐ knit on RS, purl on WS
- ● purl on RS, knit on WS
- ☒ k2tog (knit 2 stitches together)
- Ⓜ make 1
- LT (left twist)
- 2/1 LPC (2 over 1 left purl cross)
- 2/1 RPC (2 over 1 right purl cross)
- 2/2 LC (2 over 2 left cross)

49

Elegant And Feminine Knitted Scarves

Pacific Skies Scarf

Skill level: Easy

Finished scarf measures: 4½" x 60".

Materials

RED HEART® "Heart & Sole® with Aloe" yarn: 2 Balls 3970 Faded Jeans.

Elegant And Feminine Knitted Scarves

Knitting Needles: 2.75mm [US 2].

Yarn needle.

Gauge: 32 sts = 4"; 38 rows = 4" in Horseshoe Lace Pattern. Check your gauge. Use any size needles to obtain the gauge.

Abbreviations:

k = knit;

mm = millimeters;

p = purl;

st(s) = stitch(es);

tog = together;

yo = yarn over;

* or ** = repeat whatever follows the * or ** as indicated.

sk2p: slip 1, k2tog, pass slipped st over.

Horseshoe Lace Pattern (multiple of 10 sts + 1)

Rows 1 and 3 (Wrong Side): Purl.

Row 2: K1, * yo, k3, sk2p, k3, yo, k1; repeat from * across.

Row 4: P1, * k1, yo, k2, sk2p, k2, yo, k1, p1; repeat from * across.

Rows 5 and 7: * K1, p9; repeat from * to last st, k1.

Row 6: P1, * k2, yo, k1, sk2p, k1, yo, k2, p1; repeat from * across.

Row 8: P1, * k3, yo, sk2p, yo, k3, p1; repeat from * across.

Repeat Rows 1-8 for Horseshoe Lace pattern.

Pattern

Cast on 35 sts.

Beginning with a wrong side row, knit 2 rows in Garter st (knit every row).

Row 1 (Wrong Side): K2, work Row 1 of Horseshoe Lace pattern across row to last 2 sts, k2.

Keeping first and last 2 sts in Garter st for side borders, repeat Rows 1-8 of Horseshoe Lace pattern until piece measures 60" from beginning, end with Row 8.

Knit 2 rows in Garter st.

Bind off.

Weave in ends. Block to finished measurements.

Elegant And Feminine Knitted Scarves

Fluffy Rib Stitch Scarf

Skill level: Easy

Materials

RED HEART® Hygge™: 1 ball each 8406 Pearl A and 8319 Rust B

Elegant And Feminine Knitted Scarves

Susan Bates® Knitting Needles: 6mm [US 10]

Yarn needle

Gauge: 17 sts = 4" [10 cm]; 16 rows = 4" [10 cm] in Textured Rib after blocking. CHECK YOUR GAUGE. Use any size needles to obtain the gauge.

Scarf measures 5" [12.5 cm] wide x 77" [195.5 cm] long

Abbreviations

cm = centimeters;

mm = millimeters;

st(s) = stitch(es);

* = repeat whatever follows the * as indicated.

Notes

This scarf is reversible.

Scarf

With A, cast on 19 stitches.

Row 1 (Right Side): Knit 3, *purl 1, knit 3; repeat from * to end.

Row 2 (Wrong Side): Knit 1 *purl 1, knit 3; repeat from * to last 2 sts, purl 1, knit 1.

Rows 3-12: Repeat Rows 1-2, 5 times.

Cut A.

Rows 13-24: With B, repeat Rows 1-12.

Cut B.

Repeat Rows 1-24, 12 times.

Repeat Rows 1-12, once.

Bind off all sts.

Finishing

Weave in all ends. Block scarf to final measurements if desired.

Elegant And Feminine Knitted Scarves

Make It Big Super Scarf

Materials

Bernat® Softee® Chunky™ (3.5 oz/100 g; 108 yds/99 m)

Version 1: Natural (28008) 6 balls

Version 2: Wine (28532) 6 balls

Size U.S. 11 (8 mm) knitting needles or size needed to obtain gauge.

Measurement

Approx 10" [25.5 cm] wide x 100" [254 cm] long, excluding tassels.

Gauge:

11 sts and 14 rows = 4" [10 cm] in stocking st.

Abbreviations

Approx = Approximate(ly)

Beg = Begin(ning)

Dec = Decrease(ing)

Inc = Increase(ing)

K = Knit

K2tog = Knit next 2 stitches together

P = Purl

Pat = Pattern

Psso = Pass slipped stitch over

Rem = Remaining

Rep = Repeat

RS = Right side

Sl1 = Slip next stitch knitwise

St(s) = Stitch(es)

WS = Wrong side

Elegant And Feminine Knitted Scarves

Yo = Yarn over

Pattern

Cast on 27 sts.

Knit 3 rows, noting first row is WS and inc 2 sts evenly across last row. 29 sts.

Proceed in pat as follows:

1st row: (RS). K4. *P3. K3. Rep from * to last st. K1.

2nd row: K1. *P3. K3. Rep from * to last 4 sts. P3. K1.

3rd and 4th rows: As 1st and 2nd rows.

5th row: K1. *yo. Sl1. K2tog. psso. yo. K3. Rep from * to last 4 sts. yo. Sl1. K2tog. psso. yo. K1.

6th row: K1. *K3. P3. Rep from * to last 4 sts. K4.

7th row: K1. *P3. K3. Rep from * to last 4 sts. P3. K1.

8th and 9th rows: As 6th and 7th rows.

10th row: As 6th row.

11th row: K4. *yo. Sl1. K2tog. psso. yo. K3. Rep from * to last st. K1.

12th row: As 2nd row.

Elegant And Feminine Knitted Scarves

Rep last 12 rows for pat until Scarf from beg measures approx 100" [254 cm], ending on a 6th or 12th row of pat.

Next row: (RS). Knit, dec 2 sts evenly across. 27 sts.

Knit 2 rows. Cast off knitwise (WS).

Tassels (make 4)

Cut a piece of cardboard 8" [20.5 cm] wide. Wind yarn around cardboard 50 times. Break yarn leaving a long end and thread end through needle. Slip needle through all loops and tie tightly. Remove cardboard and wind yarn tightly around loops 1" [2.5 cm] below fold. Fasten securely. Cut through rem loops and trim ends evenly. Sew Tassels to each corner of Scarf at ends.

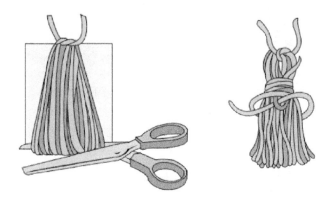

Elegant And Feminine Knitted Scarves

Basketweave Scarf

Materials

RED HEART® Super Saver Ombre™: 2 skeins 3963 Baja Blue

Susan Bates® Knitting Needles: 5.5mm [US 9]

Elegant And Feminine Knitted Scarves

Yarn needle

Gauge: 16 sts = 4" [10 cm]; 20 rows = 4" [10 cm] in Basketweave stitch. Check your gauge. Use any size needles to obtain the gauge.

Scarf measures 10" [25.5 cm] wide x 90" [229 cm] long.

Abbreviations

cm = centimeters;

k = knit;

mm = millimeters;

p = purl;

st(s) = stitch(es);

* or ** = repeat whatever follows the * or ** as indicated.

Notes

When joining new skein, pick up new skein within same color section as old skein.

Basketweave Stitch (multiple of 4 sts + 4)

Rows 1, 3 & 5 (Right Side): K3, *p2, k2; repeat from * across to last st, k1.

Rows 2, 4 & 6: P3, *k2, p2; repeat from * across to last st, p1.

Rows 7, 9 & 11: K1, *p2, k2; repeat from * across to last 3 sts, p2, k1.

Rows 8, 10 & 12: P1, *k2, p2; repeat from * across to last 3 sts, k2, p1.

Repeat Rows 1-12 for Basketweave st.

Scarf

Cast on 40 sts.

Beginning with Row 1, work in Basketweave st until piece measures 90" [229 cm] from beginning.

Bind off loosely.

Weave in ends.

Elegant And Feminine Knitted Scarves

Both Sides Knit Scarf

Skill level: Intermediate

Materials

Patons® Alpaca Blend™ (3.5 oz/100 g; 155 yds/142 m) Petunia

Elegant And Feminine Knitted Scarves

(01016) 4 balls

Size U.S. 10 (6 mm) knitting needles or size needed to obtain gauge.

Cable needle.

Measurements: Approx 6½" x 72" [16.5 x 183 cm]

Gauge: 15 sts and 20 rows = 4" [10 cm] in stocking st.

Abbreviations

Alt = Alternate(ing)

Approx = Approximately

Beg = Beginning

K = Knit

P = Purl

Pat = Pattern

Rep = Repeat

RS = Right side

St(s) = Stitch(es)

Pattern

Elegant And Feminine Knitted Scarves

Note: Scarf is reversible.

Cast on 48 sts.

1st row: (RS). (K1. P1) 24 times.

2nd and alt rows: (K1. P1) 24 times.

3rd and 5th rows: As 1st row.

7th row: *Slip 8 sts onto cable needle and leave at back of work. (K1. P1) 4 times. (K1. P1) 4 times from cable needle. (K1. P1) 4 times. Rep from * once more.

9th, 11th, 13th and 15th rows: As 1st row.

17th row: *(K1. P1) 4 times. Slip 8 sts onto cable needle and leave at front of work. (K1. P1) 4 times. (K1. P1) 4 times from cable needle.

Rep from * once more.

19th row: As 1st row.

20th row: As 2nd row.

Rep last 20 rows until work from beg measures approx 72" [183 cm], ending on a 15th row.

Cast off in pat.

Elegant And Feminine Knitted Scarves

Hollow Miters Scarf

Skill level: Intermediate

Materials

Caron® Skinny Cakes™ (8.8 oz/250 g; 795 yds/727 m) Citrón Fizz

Elegant And Feminine Knitted Scarves

(18033) 2 balls

Size U.S. 6 (4 mm) knitting needles. Size U.S. 6 (4 mm) circular knitting needle 29" [75 cm] long or size needed to obtain gauge.

Stitch markers.

Measurements

Approx 16" x 80" [40.5 x 203.5 cm], excluding fringe.

Gauge: 21 sts and 44 rows = 4" [10 cm] in garter stitch.

Abbreviations

Approx = Approximately

Beg = Begin(ning)

K2tog = Knit next 2 stitches together

Pat = Pattern

PM = Place marker

Psso =Pass slipped stitch over

St(s) = Stitch(es)

Rep = Repeat

Elegant And Feminine Knitted Scarves

RS = Right side

Sl1 = Slip next stitch knitwise

WS = Wrong side

Pattern

Note: Cable cast-on technique is used throughout.

Work back and forth across needle in rows.

To achieve random shades, separate colors for each Motif and beg 1st ball of yarn from inside of ball, start 2nd ball from outside of ball.

First Row (See diagram on next page)

First Motif: With pair of needles, cast on 37 sts.

1st row: (WS). Knit. PM on 19th st for center.

**2nd row: Knit to 1 st before center st. Remove marker. Sl1. K2tog. psso. PM on last st just made. Knit to end of row.

3rd row: Knit.

Rep last 2 rows until there are 17 sts, ending on a RS row. Cast off.**

Second Motif: Cast on 7 sts. Turn.

1st row: (RS). Pick up and knit 12 sts down left side of previous Motif.

Elegant And Feminine Knitted Scarves

Turn. Cast on 18 sts. PM on 19th st for center.

Rep from ** to ** as given above.

Third and Fourth Motifs: As Second Motif.

Second Motif

First Motif: Cast on 19 sts. Turn.

1st row: (RS). Pick up and knit 11 sts across top edge of corresponding Motif 1 row below. Turn. Cast on 7 sts. PM on 19th st for center.

Rep from ** to ** as given above.

Second Motif: Cast on 7 sts. Turn.

1st row: (RS). Pick up and knit 11 sts down left side of previous Motif of the same row. Pick up and knit 12 sts across top edge of corresponding Motif 1 row below. Turn. Cast on 7 sts. PM on 19th st for center.

Rep from ** to ** as given above.

Third and Fourth Motifs: As Second Motif.

Following Diagram, rep Second Row and join Motifs as you go, alternating balls of yarn for Motifs in checked pat to achieve random shades, until Scarf measures approx 76" [193 cm].

Elegant And Feminine Knitted Scarves

Final Row

First Motif: Cast on 19 sts. Turn.

1st row: (RS). Pick up and knit 11 sts across top edge of corresponding

Motif 1 row below. Turn. Cast on 7 sts. PM on 19th st for center.

2nd row: Knit to 1 st before center st. Remove marker. Sl1. K2tog. psso. PM on last st just made. Knit to end of row.

3rd row: Knit.

Rep last 2 rows until 3 sts rem.

Next row: Sl1. K2tog. psso. Fasten off.

Second to Fourth Motifs: 1st row: (RS). Pick up and knit 18 sts down left side of previous Motif of same row. Pick up and knit 12 sts across top edge of corresponding Motif 1 row below. Turn. Cast on 7 sts. PM on 19th st for center.

2nd row: Knit to 2 sts before center st. Sl1. K2tog. psso. Knit to end of row.

3rd row: Knit.

Rep last 2 rows until 3 sts rem.

Next row: Sl1. K2tog. psso. Fasten off.

Elegant And Feminine Knitted Scarves

Side edging: With RS facing, and circular needle, working across left side of Scarf, pick up and knit 18 sts down left side of Fourth Motif of Final Row. Do not join. Working back and forth across needle, proceed as follows: *Turn. Cast on 7 sts. Turn. Pick up and knit 11 sts down left side of next Motif. Rep from * to cast on edge of Scarf. Knit 6 rows.

Cast off knitwise (WS).

Fringe: Cut strands of yarn 16" [40.5 cm] long. Taking 4 strands together (tog), fold in half and knot into fringe across both ends of Scarf. Trim fringe evenly.

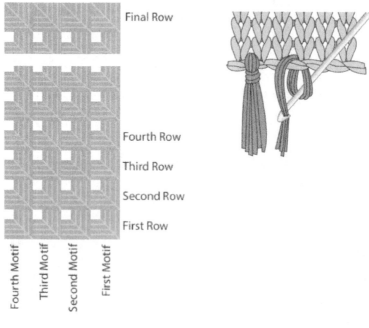

Printed in Dunstable, United Kingdom